Plan Be

'When I met Dave Andrews a few years ago, I could feel the fire burning in him. Then I heard him speak. Then I read his books. Ever since, he has been and continues to be a major inspiration for my life and work. I think *Plan Be* will be his most widely-read book yet, and introduce a new readership to this important prophetic voice – one who deserves global attention. Plan A (Aggressive, Arrogant, Angry, or Apathetic Religion) has been tried and found disgusting. It's high time for Plan Be spirituality.'

Brian McLaren, author/activist

'With gentle forcefulness Dave Andrews helps us to emancipate the Beatitudes from the too-hard list, and embrace them as prime ingredients in God's recipe for a grace-full revolution.'

Steve Bradbury, TEAR Australia and Micah Network

'The essence of Jesus' teaching is the Sermon on the Mount. Yet Christians have not taken this seriously. Dave Andrews reminds us that we edit out this teaching at our global peril.'

Tim Costello, CEO, World Vision Australia

'The Anabaptists, the Radical wing of the Reformation, believed that the Sermon on the Mount was not simply a set of ideals for a brutal world, but a way of life in following Christ and his peaceable kingdom that could be lived. This challenging book seeks to carry forward this vision into the 21st century. It is a personal and communal call to live against the tide of violence, retaliation, vengeance and unforgiveness, in order to nurture into being a world that reflects the radical grace, gentleness, love and justice of the One who uttered these words so long ago. This book is to be read, internalised and LIVED!'

Dr Charles Ringma, Emeritus Professor Mission Studies, Regent College, Vancouver, Canada.

Plan Be

Be the change
you want to see
in the world

Dave Andrews

Authentic

MILTON KEYNES ● COLORADO SPRINGS ● HYDERABAD

First published 2008 by Authentic Media
9 Holdom Avenue, Bletchley, Milton Keynes, Bucks, MK1 1QR, UK
1820 Jet Stream Drive, Colorado Springs, CO 80921, USA
OM Authentic Media, Medchal Road, Jeedimetla Village,
Secunderabad 500 055, A.P., India
www.authenticmedia.co.uk

Authentic Media is a division of IBS-STL U.K., limited by guarantee, with its
Registered Office at Kingstown Broadway, Carlisle, Cumbria CA3 0HA.
Registered in England & Wales No. 1216232. Registered charity 270162

British Library Cataloguing in Publication Data
A catalogue record for this book is available from the British Library

ISBN-13: 978-1-85078-778-5

Cover Design by fourninezero design.
Print Management by Adare
Printed and bound in Great Britain by J.H. Haynes & Co., Sparkford

Contents

The Be-Attitudes

[1]Now when he saw the crowds, he went up on a mountainside and sat down. His disciples came to him, [2]and he began to teach them, saying:

[3]'Blessed are the poor in spirit,
for theirs is the kingdom of heaven.
[4]Blessed are those who mourn,
for they will be comforted.
[5]Blessed are the meek,
for they will inherit the earth.
[6]Blessed are those who hunger and thirst for righteousness, for they will be filled.
[7]Blessed are the merciful,
for they will be shown mercy.
[8]Blessed are the pure in heart,
for they will see God.
[9]Blessed are the peacemakers,
for they will be called children of God.
[10]Blessed are those who are persecuted because of righteousness, for theirs is the kingdom of heaven.'
Matt. 5:1-10

[20]Looking at his disciples, he said:

'Blessed are you who are poor,
for yours is the kingdom of God.
[21]Blessed are you who hunger now,
for you will be satisfied.
Blessed are you who weep now,
for you will laugh.
[22]Blessed are you when men hate you,
when they exclude you and insult you
and reject your name as evil,
because of the Son of Man.
[23]Rejoice in that day and leap for joy,
because great is your reward in heaven.
For that is how their fathers treated the prophets.

[24]But woe to you who are rich,
for you have already received your comfort.
[25]Woe to you who are well fed now,
for you will go hungry.
Woe to you who laugh now,
for you will mourn and weep.
[26]Woe to you when all men speak well of you,
for that is how their fathers treated the false prophets.'
Luke 6:20–26

Plan Be:

Be the change you want to see in the world

I have become increasingly worried about how the neo-cons have set the global agenda. Those of us who have opposed the 'coalition of the willing' and protested against the killing that is being done in the name of God have apparently been rendered utterly and thoroughly impotent. Millions of us have marched in protests, signed petitions, and spoken to politicians, but with little impact. We have not changed the world.

I have come to the conclusion that it is an illusion to think we can change anyone except ourselves – and that is only possible with the help of God's Spirit! We need to pray the alternative version of the Serenity Prayer regularly

> *Lord, give me the serenity*
> *to accept the people I cannot change,*
> *the courage to change the person I can,*
> *and the wisdom to know it is me!*

But even when we realize that we are the ones who need to be changed, our aspirations for change are often simply too grandiose.

Big people can do big things. But we can only ever be big people in our own minds. In global terms, we will only ever really be little people and, as little people, we can only do little things. Great things can happen. Not as a result of little people trying to do impossibly big things; but as a result of the cumulative effect of lots of little people doing lots of the little things we can do.

As little people, we all know that there is nothing big we can do to change the world. But that doesn't mean there is nothing we can do. We can be the change we want to see in the world by simply persistently doing all the little things we wish others would do, but don't do, ourselves.

And when a majority of us in each country persistently do all the little things we wish others would do, then it will be in the self-interest of politicians who want to ensure their own political survival to develop policies that better reflect our concerns for the world.

Plan A has been to *treat others like they treat us*. On 9-11-2001, Osama Bin Laden ordered an attack on the twin towers of the World Trade Center at the heart of the American empire. As the world looked on in astonishment Bin Laden cried, 'Here is America struck by God Almighty in one of its vital organs, so that its greatest buildings are destroyed.'[1] In retaliation, George Bush ordered an attack on Osama Bin Laden in Afghanistan - and also an attack on Saddam Hussein in Iraq (who did not have any weapons of mass destruction, or anything to do with the 9-11 attack, but had tried to kill Bush senior). Bush claimed, 'God told me to strike al-Qaeda and I struck them, and then he instructed me to strike at Saddam, which I did.'[2] As a result, so far over 100,000 innocent civilians have been killed - and we are still counting.

The trouble with an eye-for-an-eye policy is that in the end it makes us blind - we are no longer able to see - let alone do - the sort of things that make for peace and love and justice.

Plan Be is to *treat others like we would like to be treated*. This is the Golden Rule.[3] Not the new materialistic version of the Golden Rule - 'Those with the gold rule' - but the old spiritual version of the Golden Rule - 'Do unto others as you would have them do unto you.' It's a call for all people - regardless of religion - to be the change we want to see in the world.

The great value of the Golden Rule is that it is acceptable not only to religious, but also to secular people. General reciprocity seems to be common to ethical systems

3

everywhere.⁴ But, while the strength of the Golden Rule is that everybody agrees with it, its weakness is that it is a bit vague as a guideline.

Which is why Jesus of Nazareth spent so much time unpacking the specific implications of the Golden Rule in his brilliant Sermon on the Mount – summarizing his suggestions in the Be-Attitudes.

The trouble is, few people who would claim to be admirers of Jesus – even among those who would call themselves believers – take the Be-Attitudes seriously as ethical guidelines. There are at least three reasons for this.

The first reason is that the Be-Attitudes are rarely taught in churches (a friend says he cannot remember ever hearing a single sermon on the Be-Attitudes in his church). If the Be-Attitudes are referred to, they are usually cited as picture-postcard spiritual promises, not as basic practical operating principles.

The second reason is that the Sermon on the Mount, which the Be-Attitudes introduce, hasn't been taught as a framework for ethics ever since the church chose to align itself with the state under the Emperor Constantine. Instead, the practical operating principles of the Sermon (like 'turn the other cheek') were set aside in order to support imperial demands (like 'take up the sword in defence of the empire').

The third reason is that when people have tried to reclaim the Sermon on the Mount as a framework for ethics, they have often misinterpreted its content and turned it into a set of idealistic but unrealistic guidelines (like 'never be angry') that make Jesus seem unreasonable or even irrational.

I hope to show you that the Sermon on the Mount in general, and the Be-Attitudes in particular, are actually an original, imaginative and brilliantly do-able set of realistic ideals that give us a way to engage a world of poverty and violence.

Let's reflect on the Be-Attitudes for a moment . . .

[3]Blessed are the poor in spirit,
for theirs is the kingdom of heaven.

[4]Blessed are those who mourn,
for they will be comforted.

[5]Blessed are the meek,
for they will inherit the earth.

[6]Blessed are those who hunger and thirst for righteousness,
for they will be filled.

[7]Blessed are the merciful,
for they will be shown mercy.

[8]Blessed are the pure in heart,
for they will see God.

[9]Blessed are the peacemakers,
for they will be called children of God.

[10]Blessed are those who are persecuted because of
righteousness,
for theirs is the kingdom of heaven.
Matt. 5:3–10

Who are the people blessed in the Be-Attitudes?

the poor – or poor in spirit
– who identify with the poor 'in spirit'

those who mourn
– who grieve over the injustice in the world

the meek
– who get angry, but who never get aggressive

those who hunger and thirst for righteousness
– who seek justice

the merciful
– who are compassionate to everyone in need

the pure in heart
– who are wholehearted in their desire to do right

the peacemakers
– who work for peace in a world at war

those persecuted for righteousness
– who suffer for just causes

What are the virtues that are blessed in each of the Be-Attitudes?

Focusing on the poor (not status or riches). *Humility*

Grieving over the injustice in the world. *Empathy*

Getting angry but not getting aggressive. *Self-restraint*

Seeking for justice (not vengeance). *Righteousness*

Extending compassion to all in need. *Mercy*

Being wholehearted in a desire to do right. *Integrity*

Working for peace in a world at war. *Non-violence*

Suffering for just causes (patiently). *Perseverance*

If we were to use the virtues blessed in the Be-Attitudes as guidelines for our lives, what kind of people do you imagine would we be?

We would identify with the poor 'in spirit'.

We would grieve over injustice in the world.

We would get angry, but never get aggressive.

We would seek to do justice, even to our enemies.

We would extend compassion to all those in need.

We would act with integrity, not just for the publicity.

We would work for peace in the midst of the violence.

We would suffer ourselves, rather than inflict suffering.

In the Be-Attitudes, Jesus gives us a set of clear ethical guidelines that can help us become the people-that-be against the powers-that-be.

In the next eight sections, I want to walk you through each of the eight Be-Attitudes, one by one, and show you how they can change your life.

1

Blessed are
the poor
and all those
who are with them
in spirit

Blessed are the poor in spirit, for
theirs is the kingdom of heaven.
(Matt. 5:3)

When we want to reflect on the Beatitudes we usually turn to Matthew's version, quoted above. But to appreciate the full significance of what Jesus is saying, we also need to turn to Luke's version (Luke 6:20-24), which says: 'Blessed are you who are poor, for yours is the kingdom of God. But woe to you who are rich, for you have already received your comfort.'

When we read Matthew's version, most of us feel comforted. Because we feel 'poor in spirit', and Jesus' promise of blessing is of great comfort to all of us who struggle. But when we read Luke's version, if you are anything like me, you will feel very uncomfortable indeed. Because, though none of us like to admit we are rich, (the 'rich' are 'people who have more than us'), we know deep down that in global terms even those of us on social security in capitalist economies are comparatively rich, for our income is in the top 20 per cent in the world! (If you don't believe me, go to

10

www.globalrichlist.com, enter your income, and check where you stand financially in relation to the rest of the world's population.) So we read Jesus' affirmation of the poor – and condemnation of the rich – with great personal discomfort. It is very confronting stuff indeed.

When we read other passages in Scripture, in the hope of finding a more accommodating gospel, we are confronted with the same uncompromising message everywhere we turn. His mother Mary said that through her son Jesus, God would 'fill the hungry with good things' and 'send the rich away empty' (Luke 1:53).

In Jesus, God 'became poor' (2 Cor. 8:9) and preached 'good news to the poor' (Luke 4:18). He was 'born in a manger' (Luke 2:7). He had 'nowhere to lay his head' (Luke 9:58). He didn't have any money in his pocket. When he needed a coin, he even had to ask somebody else to give him one (Mark 12:15). He constantly associated with poor people – embracing outcasts and healing the sick (Matt. 11:4–5) – and courageously advocated for poor people – driving out the money-changers in the temple who, no doubt, exploited them in the same way as they had exploited his parents years before (Mark 11:15–17).

Jesus criticized people's obsession with riches (Matt. 6:19) and ridiculed rich people (Matt. 6:25–9). He used to tell a story about an investor who had a successful business, calling him a 'rich fool' (Luke 12:16). He asked: 'What good is it . . . to gain the whole world, and yet lose your soul?' (Luke 9:25).

Jesus unpacked what he had in mind about the rich losing their souls in a scandalous parable. He said

> There was a rich man who was dressed in purple and fine linen and lived in luxury every day. At his gate was laid a beggar named Lazarus, covered with sores and longing to eat what fell from the rich man's table. Even the dogs came and licked his sores . . . The beggar died and the angels carried him to Abraham's side. The rich man also died and was buried. In hell, where he was in torment, he looked up and saw Abraham far away, with Lazarus by his side. So he called to him, 'Father Abraham, have pity on me and send Lazarus to dip the tip of his finger in water and cool my tongue, because I am in agony in this fire.' But Abraham replied, 'Son, remember in your lifetime you received your good things, while Lazarus received bad things, but now he is comforted here and you are in agony' (Luke 16:19-25).

This parable illustrates Jesus' passionate commitment to the *'upside-down society'* he believed God would one day establish. A society which is the exact opposite of our own – the first are last, the last are first, and the fate of the rich and the poor are reversed.

To the great consternation of the key stakeholders in the status quo, with God's help, the early Christians were 'able to do immeasurably more' than one might have imagined they would have been able to do, to make Jesus' dream a

reality (Eph. 3:20). They chose the 'things that are not' –
to nullify 'the things that are' (1 Cor. 1:26,28) and time and
time again they helped 'foolish' people to confuse the
'wise', and 'weak' people confound the 'strong' (1 Cor.
1:26) in their quest to develop inclusive and egalitarian
communities of faith in the midst of religious traditions
which had previously disenfranchised them. In fact, they
succeeded to such an extent that one horrified observer
is recorded as saying – 'these people have turned the
whole world upside-down'! (Acts 17:6)

In the light of these scriptures, it is very clear why the
gospel of Jesus is 'good news for the poor'. The poor are
blessed because, in the 'upside-down society' that is the
kingdom of God, the poor have a place of honour they can
find nowhere else; and God says that 'the kingdom of God
is theirs'. They are blessed not because they are poor but
because even though they are poor, they are loved; and
because they are loved, people will share their wealth with
them, and help them meet their basic needs. When the
early Christians were 'one in heart', 'No-one claimed that
any of their possessions was their own, but they shared
everything they had', so 'There were no needy persons
among them' (Acts 4:32–4).

What is not so clear is how the gospel of Jesus can be good
news to the rich – like you and me. When a rich man came
to Jesus and asked him what he could do to recover his
soul and discover eternal life, Jesus said: 'Sell everything
you have and give to the poor . . . Then come, follow me'
(Luke 18:22). Now, for those of us who are rich, it is hard

to see where the good news is in that for us. Which makes sense, because there isn't any. The good news in it is for the poor – who are going to get everything we've got. But there is good news in it for us too. It's just we are so shocked about the demand to 'sell everything and give it to the poor . . . Then come, follow me', we don't hear Jesus say 'and you will have treasure in heaven'! But he does (Luke 18:22). And it is our salvation (Luke 18:28–30). The poor are indeed blessed. But, so also are all those of us who are with the poor 'in spirit'.

2

Blessed are those who mourn

who wail, lament
and cry out loud

Blessed are those who mourn,
for they will be comforted.
(Matt. 5:4)

According to those in the know, the Greek word used in this phrase to describe 'mourning' is the strongest in the Greek language. It signifies the devastating grief of a lover over the death of their dearly beloved – the experience of deep, profound, poignant, painful, sorrow.

There is certainly a lot of death and dying in the world for us to grieve over. While the top 20 per cent of the world's population have more than 80 per cent of the world's total income and live lives of unparalleled luxury, the bottom 20 per cent of the world's population try to survive on less than 1.5 per cent of the world's income and are condemned to live lives characterized by cycles of deprivation and despair. Because they cannot access their fair share of the world's income, many, in desperation, sell their labour for a pittance. More than 250 million children work for as little as 25 cents a day. As a last resort, many even have to sell their bodies. More than a million children are forced into prostitution every year. Millions of children under the age of 15 are developing HIV and dying of AIDS, and more than 25,000 people die unnecessarily from easily preventable causes every day of every week of every year.

However, though there is much to grieve over, not everyone mourns the current state of the world. What we feel depends on what we see and hear, and what we see and hear depends on where we stand in the world. If we identify with the top 20 per cent of the world's population who are 'well fed' and 'laugh' (Luke 6:25), we will probably 'rejoice with those who rejoice' (Rom. 12:15). It is only if we identify with the other 80 per cent of the world's population – especially the bottom 20 per cent – who 'go hungry' and 'weep' themselves to sleep (Luke 6:25) that we will actually 'mourn with those who mourn' (Rom. 12:15).

Scripture suggests that God identifies with all people he has made in his image – both rich and poor (Gen. 1:26-7); but God has a special place in his heart for the poor who are treated so heartlessly (Prov. 14:31). When God comes in Jesus, he makes it very clear where he stands. He says: 'Whatever you do to one of the least' – one of those that most of you consider the least – the marginalized, distressed, disabled, and disadvantaged – 'you do it to me' (Matt. 25:40). God says that whenever you crush his people contemptuously – he takes it personally – it's as if you were actually crushing him – and he grieves about it deeply. He says 'my people are crushed, I am crushed; I mourn, and horror grips me' (Jer. 8:21-2).

17

As God's people, we are called to love the world as God does, and given the state of the world, all those who love the world as God does will 'mourn' horribly over the state of the world as God does. As we sympathize with God and empathize with our neighbours who are in pain – as we are expected to – we will inevitably be moved towards 'com-passion' – or 'a deep sense of shared pain' (Luke 10:27). When it comes to compassion, Jesus is our supreme example. 'When he saw the crowds, he had compassion on them, because they were harassed and helpless, like sheep without a shepherd' (Matt. 9:36).

Three phases of mourning are associated with a compassionate response to a world in pain.[5]

The first phase is *wailing* – agonizing with the pain – either as a victim or as one who loves the victim. Jesus wailed with Mary over the death of her brother Lazarus.

> When Jesus saw her weeping, and the Jews who had come along with her also weeping, he was deeply moved in spirit and troubled. 'Where have you laid him?' he asked. 'Come and see, Lord,' they replied. Jesus wept (John 11:33-5).

The second phase is *lamenting* – analysing the pain, its tragic causes and catastrophic consequences – as the psalmists did in the psalms of lament. Jesus lamented over Jerusalem.

> As he approached Jerusalem and saw the city, he wept over it and said, 'If you, even you, had only

18

known on this day what would bring you peace
– but now it is hidden from your eyes. The days
will come upon you when your enemies will build
an embankment against you and encircle you and
hem you in on every side. They will dash you to
the ground, you and the children within your
walls. They will not leave one stone on another,
because you did not recognize the time of God's
coming to you' (Luke 19:41-4).

The third phase is *crying out loud*: criticizing the groups
and organizations that are the perpetrators of pain in our
society - like the prophets did - so that the public are
forced to confront the issues involved. Jesus cried out loud
against the merchants in the temple.

When it was almost time for the Jewish Passover,
Jesus went up to Jerusalem. In the temple courts
he found men selling cattle, sheep and doves, and
others sitting at tables exchanging money. So he
made a whip out of cords, and drove all from the
temple area, both sheep and cattle; he scattered
the coins of the moneychangers and overturned
their tables. To those who sold doves he said, 'Get
these out of here! How dare you turn my Father's
house into a market!' (John 2:13-16)

Jesus does not bless those who are happy with the present
state of affairs. He blesses those who 'mourn'.

3

**Blessed are
the meek**
who practise
self-restraint
and self-control

*Blessed are the meek, for they
will inherit the earth.*
(Matt. 5:5)

In the ancient world in which Jesus lived, the concept of meekness was very different from today. Today, the word 'meek' is often used as a synonym for 'weak'. So we often think of a meek person as a weak person – a wimp, a wuss, a gutless wonder – a scrawny, cowardly individual. But in Jesus' day, the word 'meek' was often used to connote quiet, controlled, internal strength of character, which opponents would interpret as a sign of weakness at their own peril.

The word *prau* – which we translate as 'meek' – actually had two separate but interrelated meanings. The first meaning was neither too much anger, nor too little anger, but just the right amount of righteous indignation to address any grievous wrong. The second meaning was separate from, but related to, the first. It was used about domesticating wild horses, harnessing the explosive potency of primal, spirited power.[6]

So when Jesus talked about the meek, he was talking about people who practised spirited but non-reactive self-restraint and powerful but non-violent self-control in the face of violent provocation.

There is great danger in getting angry. When we get angry, we want to hit back at people who have hurt us, or hurt those whom we love. When we hit back, we are tempted to hurt them as they hurt us. We call them names, which dehumanize them or demonize them, and then set out to destroy them.

On 9-11-2001, Osama Bin Laden ordered an attack on the twin towers of the World Trade Center at the heart of the 'Satanic' empire, killing more than 2,000 innocent Americans. In retaliation, George Bush ordered an attack on Osama Bin Laden in Afghanistan and an attack on the tyrant Saddam Hussein in Iraq, leading to the deaths of over a 100,000 innocent civilians – and counting.

So it is not surprising that Jesus said:

> You have heard that it was said . . . 'Do not murder, and anyone who murders will be subject to judgment.' But I tell you that anyone who is angry with his brother will be subject to judgment. Again anyone who says to his brother, 'Raca', ['I spit on you'] is answerable to the Sanhedrin. But anyone who says, 'You fool!' will be in danger of the fire of hell (Matt. 5:21–2).

However, while Jesus says there is grave danger in getting mad and calling people names, Jesus does *not* say that we should not be angry, or never call anyone a fool. There is plenty of evidence Jesus got angry (Matt. 21:12–17) and called the Pharisees fools (Matt. 23:17). His statements here are not prescriptive, but descriptive. He depicts a violent cycle of action and reaction we can get stuck in, if we are not careful, by being annoyed with one another and insulting one another. Yet, he does not tell his disciples not to be angry; he tells them – as Paul reminds us – to 'be angry but do not sin' (Eph. 4:26).[7]

Jesus shows us how we can be angry 'yet without sin' at the tomb of Lazarus. John says that when Jesus was confronted with his friend's death, he was 'deeply moved' (John 11:33,38). The word we translate as 'deeply moved' is *embrimaomai*. It means to 'snort in spirit'. It is the word used to describe a stallion, rearing up on its hind legs, tearing the air with its hooves and snorting before it charges into battle.[8] By using this word repeatedly, John is saying Jesus got really, really 'wild' about the needless death of his friends and was 'mad' enough to do something about it, even though it looked impossible.

But, unlike many of us when we get mad, Jesus made sure he channelled his rage constructively. He didn't react and return evil for evil. He acted proactively, 'overcoming evil with good' (Rom. 12:21).

Now, the only way we will ever be able to act proactively, like Jesus did, is if we practise self-control to such a degree that we do not react, but respond with self-restraint – regardless of the way others treat us. Jesus says we can practise proactive self-control by learning to 'turn the other cheek', 'go the second mile' and give people the 'shirt off our back'. He says,

> If someone strikes you on the right cheek, turn to them the other also and if someone wants to sue you and take your tunic, give them your cloak as well. If someone forces you to go one mile, go with them two miles. Give to the one who asks you, and do not turn away from the one who wants to borrow from you (Matt. 5:39-42).

Jesus says, 'do unto others as you would have them do unto you' (Matt. 7:12). Do not treat others as they treat you – nor as they might treat you – but as you would like to be treated – regardless of the way that they may treat you.

> 'You have heard: . . . "Love your neighbour and hate your enemy." But I tell you: Love your enemies and pray for those who persecute you that you may be sons (and daughters) of your Father in heaven. He causes his sun to rise on the evil and the good, and sends rain on the righteous and the unrighteous . . . Be perfect, therefore, as your heavenly Father is perfect.' (Matt. 5:44-8).

Jesus says, 'blessed are the meek, for they will inherit the earth' advisedly (Matt. 5:4). Because if we are 'meek' – like our sister Gladys Staines, whose story is told here – and 'love our enemies' – there is more than enough room in the world for all of us – friends and enemies alike. But if we are not 'meek' - and want to bomb the hell out of our enemies like our misguided brother George Bush - there will be no earth left for us to inherit.

A widow shows us the way forward

Gladys and Graham Staines were Australian Christians, married in 1983, who went to India to work with the poor, and particularly with people with leprosy. They settled in Baripada in Orissa, where they worked in a leprosy home which provided medical treatment to leprosy patients, taught them skills in hand weaving and in making grass products, and ran its own dairy farm. The people in the town of Baripada often came to the home for medical treatment too.

Graham was fluent in the Oriya, Santhali and Ho languages and assisted in the translation of the Bible into the Ho language. Gladys made sure that their three children (one daughter, Esther, and two sons, Philip and Timothy) also learnt to speak the local language and played with the local children - including the children of leprosy patients.

Swami Agnivesh, a famous Arya Samaj Hindu leader, commented:

> It is a mark of the Staines family's total identification with the local people that they could speak Santhali. What a refreshing contrast to the ways of our elite who are eager to leave this country. Unlike the Staines family, they disdain to speak local languages and it is anybody's guess if they would allow their children to play with the children of leprosy patients![9]

Graham and his colleagues also visited Christians in remote areas, conducting Bible studies and teaching about health and hygiene. On 23 January 1999, during one such visit, Graham and his sons, Philip and Timothy, slept in their station wagon. Shortly after midnight, their car was set on fire by a group of Hindu militants, furious about the Staineses' evangelistic activities. Graham and the boys were burnt alive.

From the instant Gladys got news of the deaths, she publicly offered the killers her forgiveness. She says,

> It wasn't something I had thought about. But when I heard that the family was dead, I told Esther, my daughter: 'We'll forgive those who killed them, won't we?' And she said: 'Yes, Mummy, we will.'
>
> Two weeks later someone approached me at her school and said: 'I can't understand how you can forgive.' My daughter later told me: 'Mummy, I can't understand how they can't understand why we have forgiven.' That was when I understood how deeply the teachings of Christ had penetrated within my daughter. Forgiveness brings healing. It allows the other person a chance to start life afresh. If I have something against you and I forgive you, the bitterness leaves me. It also allows you to accept the forgiveness and move on. Forgiveness liberates both the forgiver and the forgiven.[10]
>
> I have no hatred for anyone.[11]

Gladys did not leave India. She continued her work at the leprosy home while her daughter completed her studies at Hebron at Ooty, only returning to Australia when her daughter moved there to study medicine.

Her response impressed others. Swami Agnivesh says:

> Though wounded in her soul by the barbarity inflicted on her dear husband and darling children, she refused to allow her mind to be tainted by hate. She was quick to forgive her husband's killers. Her prayer was that the love of God that inspired her husband may touch their hearts also. She had the spiritual magnanimity to recognise that those who become mad with hate are also children of God, and that they too deserve forgiveness. Her 13-year-old daughter, Esther, thanked God for her father's love for the people he treated - people afflicted with leprosy - and for finding him worthy to die for Christ. Can responses such as these fail to melt even the most hardened hearts?[12]

The response of people in India to Gladys and Esther's inspirational example has been remarkable. People all over the country have rallied around them. Thousands have written letters of support, and well-known Hindu leaders have led unity marches, demonstrating their solidarity with Gladys and Esther as Christians. In 2002, peace activists gave Gladys the prestigious Gandhi Community Harmony Award, and in 2005, the President of India,

Abdul Kalam - who is a Muslim - presented Gladys with the illustrious *Padmashri* Award, the highest civilian honour in the republic, in recognition of her distinguished service to the nation.

Swami Agnivesh says:

> It is through people like Mrs Staines that religion finds its true expression.

4

Blessed are those who seek righteousness

to do right
by others

*Blessed are those who hunger
and thirst for righteousness,
for they will be filled.*
(Matt. 5:6)

Many of us interpret Jesus' blessing upon those 'who hunger and thirst for righteousness', as a particular benediction for those of us who zealously seek personal piety. However, the word that we translate as 'righteousness', which Jesus uses in this blessing, indicates he is commending those who fervently seek social justice in this world, rather than personal piety that is not of this world.

The fact that Jesus bestowed his blessing upon those 'who hunger and thirst for justice' should come as no great surprise to those of us who know the Scripture. The pursuit of justice is a core theme in the Bible, and the words used for 'justice' recur over a thousand times in the Old and the New Testaments.

For Jesus, the pursuit of justice involved five different tasks: confronting injustice in society, delivering the poor from exploitation by the rich, liberating the powerless from oppression by the powerful, freeing people from the cycles of violence and counter-violence which are a constant threat to vulnerable populations, and creating just communities which are intentionally committed to including outcasts.[13]

Many people say that Jesus said a lot about love, but very little about political, economic and social justice. But Jesus constantly confronted the injustice in his society. the Synoptic Gospels record 40 instances – not counting the parallel passages – of Jesus specifically and repeatedly confronting both Roman and Jewish authorities with the injustices they perpetrated in Israel.

Jesus followed on from John the Baptist in denouncing the exploitation of the poor by the rich. John told the armed forces:

> 'Don't extort money and don't accuse people falsely – be content with your pay.' And he told the tax collectors: 'Don't collect any more than you are required to.' He said: 'The man with two tunics should share with him who has none, and the one who has food should do the same' (Luke 3:11–14).

Jesus confronted Zacchaeus, an infamous tax collector, personally about his extortion. As a result of this encounter, Zacchaeus promised Jesus to give 'half of my possessions to the poor', and 'if I have cheated anybody out of anything, I will pay back four times the amount' (Luke 19:8).

Jesus not only consistently denounced the oppression of the powerless by the powerful, he also actively advocated liberation of disempowered groups of people through the empowerment of the Spirit. Jesus attacked the key religious leaders of the day, as 'lovers of money' (Luke 16:14-15), who would maintain a façade of sanctity, by saying long prayers in public, but would 'devour widows' houses'. When he saw a widow 'put everything - all she had to live on' - into the collection box, Jesus condemned the temple for extorting the last coin from the kind of person it was set up to protect (Mark 12:38-44). Jesus broke the monopoly on forgiveness that the temple had developed through the sacrificial system it controlled. He did this by baptizing people in the Spirit and giving them the authority to forgive sins. 'Receive the Holy Spirit,' Jesus said; and 'If you forgive anyone his sins, they are forgiven' (John 20:22-3).

Jesus advocated communities with leadership that would serve the people rather than oppress them. He told his disciples:

> You know that the rulers of the Gentiles lord it over them, and their high officials exercise authority over them. Not so with you. Instead, whoever wants to become great among you must be your servant, and whoever wants to be first must be your slave—just as the Son of Man did not come to be served, but to serve, and to give his life as a ransom for many (Matt. 20:25-8).

34

Jesus demonstrated active, radical, sacrificial non-violence that would free people from the cycles of violence and counter-violence. He said

> I am the good shepherd. The good shepherd lays down his life for the sheep. The hired hand is not the shepherd who owns the sheep. So when he sees the wolf coming, he abandons the sheep and runs away. Then the wolf attacks the flock and scatters it. The man runs away because he is a hired hand and cares nothing for the sheep. I am the good shepherd . . . and I lay down my life for the sheep (John 10:11–15).

> All who ever came before me were thieves and robbers . . . I am the gate; whoever enters through me will be saved. He will come in and go out, and find pasture. The thief comes only to steal and kill and destroy; I have come that they may have life, and have it to the full (John 10:9–10).

Jesus turned to his friends and said: 'Greater love has no one than this, that he lay down his life for his friends' (John 15:13).

Jesus created communities that were committed to doing justice to the marginalized and disadvantaged. The dominant value of Jewish society was purity – but the dominant value of Jesus was inclusivity. While the Jews despised Gentiles, Jesus declared, 'my house will be called a house . . . for all nations' (Mark 11:17). While the

Pharisees ostracized sinners, Jesus invited outcasts to his parties (Mark 2:16). Jesus said

> When you give a luncheon or dinner, do not invite your friends, your brothers (sisters) or relatives, or your rich neighbours; if you do, they may invite you back and so you will be repaid. But when you give a banquet, invite the poor, the crippled, the lame, the blind, and you will be blessed. Although they cannot repay you, you will be repaid at the resurrection of the righteous (Luke 14:12-14).

The world is cursed by the fact that there are so many of us who witness injustice but do nothing about it. Jesus says that: those who bless others - by seeking to do justice to them - will be blessed themselves.

5

**Blessed are
the merciful**
who treat others
like themselves

Blessed are the merciful,
for they will be shown mercy.
(Matt. 5:7)

Jesus blesses those who seek justice, but reminds us that true justice always needs to be full of mercy. As far as Jesus is concerned, it is impossible for any of us to do justice to one another unless we show the same kind of mercy to others as we would hope – and pray – for others to extend to us in our need.

Jesus said we can summarize all the laws written in holy scriptures, and all of the words uttered by godly prophets, in two commandments – one of which is 'love your neighbour as yourself' (Matt. 22:39). So true spirituality means you should 'do unto others as you would have them do unto you' (Matt. 7:12).

In the light of this truth, it is not surprising we can find a reciprocal 'Mercy Rule' in all major religions.

The Mercy Rule in Major Religions

Hinduism
'Never do to others what would pain you.'
Panchatantra 3.104

Buddhism
'Hurt not others with that which hurts yourself.'
Udana 5.18

Zoroastrianism
'Do not to others what is not well for oneself.'
Shayast-na-shayast 13.29

Jainism
'One who neglects existence disregards their own existence.' *Mahavira*

Confucianism
'Do not impose on others what you do not yourself desire.' *Analects 12.2*

Taoism
'Regard your neighbour's loss or gain as your own loss or gain.' *Tai Shang Kan Ying Pien*

Baha'i
'Desire not for anyone the things you would not desire for yourself.' *Baha'Ullah 66*

Judaism
'What is hateful to you do not do to your neighbour.'
Talmud, Shabbat, 31a

Christianity
'Do unto others as you would have them do unto you.'
Matthew 7:12

Islam
'Do unto all people as you would they should do to you.' *Mishkat-el-Masabih*

Sikhism
'Treat others as you would be treated yourself.'
Adi Granth

In Jainism the call is *descriptive*. 'One who neglects existence disregards their own existence.' In Taoism the Mercy Rule is *instructive*. 'Regard your neighbour's loss or gain as your own loss or gain.' In Hinduism, Buddhism, Zoroastrianism, Confucianism, Judaism and Baha'i the Mercy Rule is *imperative* and is framed *in negative terms*. 'Never do to others what would pain you.' 'Hurt not others with that which hurts yourself.' 'What is hateful to you do not do to your neighbour.' 'Do not impose on others what you do not yourself desire'. 'Desire not for anyone the things you would not desire for yourself.' While in Christianity, Islam and Sikhism the Mercy Rule is *imperative* and is framed *in positive terms*. 'Do unto others as you would have them do unto you'. 'Do unto all people as you would they should do to you.' 'Treat others as you would be treated yourself.' *People of all religions – or none – all over the world know that there are no short cuts; that there are no quick fixes; and that we cannot hope to do justice, if we do not practice the Mercy Rule, and 'do unto others as we would have them do unto us'.*

Empathy is the heart of mercy. It is the capacity to feel how others feel. It is in empathizing with potential victims - people in danger or distress - and feeling how they might feel so that we can be motivated to refrain from harming them, and even to consider helping them, like Jesus did.

One day Jesus was teaching, when a whole crowd of noisy people arrived dragging a woman who had been caught red-handed having an affair. They wanted Jesus to pass judgment on her. According to Jewish law, if this woman was an adulteress, she was meant to be executed by stoning. Jesus had gone on public record as being totally opposed to affairs. As a matter of fact, Jesus had gone much further than the law, and claimed that, if anyone even entertained the idea of having an affair with someone that they weren't married to, they were already an adulterer in their hearts. So, when the woman was caught, red-handed, having an affair, it seemed an open-and-shut case. The woman had been caught in the act. The law required death – by stoning – straight away. Surely Jesus, by his own standards, would have to judge the woman guilty of 'adultery' and condemn her to death as an adulteress (John 8:1-6).

When asked for his verdict Jesus said to the crowd of men around him, 'Let those of you without sin cast the first stone at her.' He then stooped and wrote something in the dust on the ground with his finger, leaving the men, baying for the woman's blood, to make their own judgment (John 8:7-8). The men eventually made their judgment and left – one by one – 'from the oldest to the youngest' and the woman was left alone with Jesus. 'Has no-one condemned you?' he asked. 'No one, sir,' she said. Then Jesus made his judgement. He said, 'neither do I condemn you. Just don't do it again' (John 8:9-11).

Jesus encouraged people to make judgments – but only judgments tempered with mercy by empathy.

When the disciples asked how often they were required to show mercy to someone, Jesus said

> If your brother or sister sins, rebuke them, and if
> they repent, forgive them. If they sin against you
> seven times a day and seven times come back to
> you and say, 'I repent,' forgive them (Luke 17:3-4).

On another occasion he said to them, 'Actually, make that, not seven times, but seventy times seven!' (Matt. 18:22), and when the disciples asked why they should be expected to forgive people *ad infinitum*, Jesus said to them

> If you forgive people when they sin against you,
> your Heavenly Father will forgive you. But if you
> do not forgive people their sins, your Heavenly
> Father will not forgive your sin (Matt. 6:14-15).

When we are confronted with HIV/AIDS, which can be transmitted by illicit sex and drug use, it is all too easy to judge without mercy, blame the victims, and condemn them to perdition. But James reminds us, it is unjust for us to expect to receive mercy if we do not show mercy to others. He said: 'judgment without mercy will be shown to anyone who has not been merciful' (Jas. 2:13).

'Blessed are the merciful,' Jesus said, 'for they will be shown mercy' as they show mercy (Matt. 5:7).

The table in this chapter is taken from Hans Kung, 'A Global Ethic' in *A Parliament of Souls*, edited by Michael Tobias, Jane Morrison, Bettina Gray, KQED Books, San Francisco, 1995, p125.

6

**Blessed are
the pure in heart**
who really
clean up their act

Blessed are the pure in heart,
for they shall see God.
(Matt. 5:8)

Jesus encouraged people to be righteous (Matt. 5:6). In fact, he consistently challenged ordinary people to be more righteous than the Pharisees - the most righteous people of his time (Matt. 5:20). He said that the problem with the Pharisees was that they 'clean the outside of the cup but inside (they) are full of wickedness' (Luke 11:39). He wanted people to be 'pure - or clean - in heart' (Matt. 5:8).

The word Jesus used for 'pure - or clean - in heart' is recorded as *katharos,* a word that was used to describe winnowed wheat and unadulterated wine. It suggests unmixed motives. Jesus said that it was essential for anyone who really wanted to be righteous 'to clean the inside of the cup' thoroughly (Matt. 23:26). 'Be perfect,' he said, 'as your heavenly Father is perfect' (Matt. 5:48).

Faced with Jesus' expectations, the obvious question followers of Jesus are forced to answer is: How in the world does Jesus expect us to be able to clean up our act to such an extent that we can be perfect?

I think part of the answer to the question is in being clear about what Jesus meant by being 'perfect'. The adjective used here is *telios*, which is derived from the noun *telos*, which means 'purpose'. Thus what Jesus is expecting in terms of 'perfection' is that we 'realize our potential'. We are created in the image of God to reflect the love of God in our lives as realistically as we can. So, as far as Jesus is concerned, for us to be perfect we need to let the light of the love of God so shine in our lives, that people will see our 'good deeds' and 'glorify our Father in heaven' (Matt. 5:16, NASB).[14]

Jesus' expectations of us have nothing to do with abstract faultlessness, and everything to do with concrete faithfulness. What is not so clear is how we can practise concrete faithfulness.

Most Christian scholars suggest that at least a part of Jesus' answer to this question is discipleship, following carefully in the footsteps of the master and incorporating his virtues into our character. For it is in imitating Jesus that all of us can learn how to embody the virtues he incarnated.

In the Sermon on the Mount, the traits Jesus advocated we incorporate into our character include humility, empathy, self-control, righteousness, mercy, integrity, non-violence and perseverance.

Some Christian scholars, like Dallas Willard, believe that what Jesus was saying in the Sermon on the Mount was that his disciples needed to learn to distinguish between the higher ideals he advocated and the lower ideals his society advocated, and be committed to practising his higher ideals. Thus, for example, Willard says Jesus calls his disciples to practise the high ideal of 'no anger' rather than the lower ideal of 'no murder'.[15]

The lower ideal of Jewish tradition	The higher ideal of Jesus' mission
You have heard it was said to the people long ago, '*Do not murder*', and 'anyone who murders will be subject to judgement' (Matt. 5:21).	But I tell you that anyone who is *angry* with his brother (or sister) will be subject to judgement. (For example) anyone who says to his brother (or sister), 'Raca,' is answerable to the Sanhedrin and anyone who says, 'You fool!' will be in danger of the fire of hell (Matt. 5:22).

The trouble with this perspective is that the higher ideal advocated is not only completely unrealistic but also unbiblical. None of our examples of perfection in the Bible – not even Jesus – practised 'no anger' as a principle. Not only did Jesus get angry (Matt. 21:12-17), he occasionally called his opponents 'fools' (Matt. 23:17).

Christian scholars like Glen Stassen and David Gushee believe that, while saintly Christian scholars like Dallas Willard are right in asserting what Jesus was saying in the Sermon on the Mount was that his disciples needed to be able to distinguish between the higher ideals he advocated and the lower ideals his society advocated, they have been wrong when it comes to identifying these higher ideals. They have identified unrealistic ideals that Jesus never advocated, and those of us who have tried to practise them have experienced profound disappointment.

If we read the Sermon on the Mount carefully, we will notice when Jesus contrasts society's ideals with his ideals, he doesn't simply state society's lower ideals and then his 'higher ideals' second. Instead, he states society's ideals first; then he identifies the vicious cycles of unresolved problems that society's ideals do not deal with, and finally he presents his higher ideals, which alone can solve the unresolved problems of the world. Jesus' higher ideals – which are actually very realistic but incredibly creative transformative initiatives – are to be found, not in his second statements, but in his third set of statements.

It is clear that the emphasis here is not on the second point but on the third point. The imperative we are to take to heart is not an unrealistic 'no anger' policy, but a creative response to conflict resolution.

If we are to be pure in heart according to the Sermon on the Mount, we need to reflect on the first set of points, consider the second set of points, and always act on the third set of points Jesus makes.

Traditional Norms	Vicious Cycle	Transforming Initiatives
You have heard it was said to the people long ago, 'Do not murder', and 'anyone who murders will be subject to judgment' (Matt. 5:21).	But I tell you that anyone who is angry with his brother (or sister) will be subject to judgment. Anyone who says to his brother (or sister), 'Raca,' is answerable to the Sanhedrin and anyone who says, 'You fool!' will be in danger of the fire of hell (Matt. 5:22).	Therefore, if you are offering your gift at the altar and there remember that your brother (or sister) has something against you, leave your gift there in front of the altar. First go and be reconciled to your brother (or sister); then come and offer your gift. Settle matters (or make friends) quickly with your adversary who is taking you to court (Matt. 5:23–6).
The Old Imperatives	**Descriptive / Not Prescriptive**	**The New Imperatives**[16]

We are in a big mess. Jesus says that parading our piety, praying publicly and condemning other people – while nursing our lust, being angry and abusive, returning evil for evil, and abandoning our commitments to one another – only makes things worse. He tells us to clean up our act. We need to develop an unpretentious spirituality that quietly deals with temptation, gently encourages everyone in their desire to do right, loves all people – including those who hate us – and works creatively for real change in the world, for 'heaven on earth', by turning the other cheek, taking the plank out of our own eye and 'being reconciled' with all of our estranged brothers and sisters in the human family.

Jesus says that all those who 'clean up their act' – practising his idealistic-but-realistic initiatives – will see God. They certainly will. The 'pure in heart' will see God reflected in everything they say and do.

The tables in this chapter are taken from *Kingdom Ethics* by Glen H. Stassen and David P. Gushee. Copyright © 2003 by Glen H. Stassen and David P. Gushee. Used with permission of InterVarsity Press, PO Box 1400, Downers Grove, IL 60515.

Traditional Norms	Vicious Cycle	Transforming Initiatives
1. Don't kill	But being so angry you're abusive can be brutal too	Go, be reconciled
2. Don't commit adultery	But a slow-burn lust is adultery in your heart	So remove yourself from the temptation (Mark 9:43–50)
3. You can divorce	But divorce usually involves infidelity	Be reconciled (1 Cor. 7–11)
4. Don't swear falsely	But taking any oath suggests making false claims	Let your 'Yes' be 'Yes' and your 'No' be 'No'
5. Take an eye for an eye, and a tooth for a tooth	But retaliating entails returning evil for evil	Turn the other cheek
6. Love your neighbour and hate your enemy	But hating enemies doesn't deal with enmity	Love your enemies, bless those who curse you
7. Contributing publicly	Is parading your charity not practising generosity	Give without advertising it

Traditional Norms	Vicious Cycle	Transforming Initiatives
8. Fasting publicly	Is parading your piety not practising sincerity	Fast without publicizing it
9. Praying publicly	Is parading your religiosity not practising spirituality	Pray authentically in secret
10. Lots of prayer	Is simply repeating a lot of empty sacred phrases	Make the Lord's Prayer the prayer of your heart
11. Pile up treasures on earth (Luke 12:16–31)	But thieves break in and steal	Store up treasures in heaven
12. No one can serve two different masters	It's impossible to serve God and money at the same time	So seek the kingdom of God and don't worry about money
13. Do not judge lest you be judged	If you judge you'll be judged by the very same standards	So take the plank out of your own eye before you take the speck out of your neighbour's
14. Do not throw your pearls before swine	They will trample on them and then tear you to pieces	The only one you can totally entrust yourself to – is God![17]

7

**Blessed are the
peacemakers**
who are the true
children of God

Blessed are the peacemakers,
for they will be called
the children of God.
(Matt. 5:9)

Many devotees of many different religious traditions claim to be the 'children of God'. And many of these so-called 'children of God' slaughter their brothers and sisters in the name of God. Christians, Muslims and Jews use the violence advocated in the Hebrew Bible to justify their violence. After all, they say, Moses says, 'if there is serious injury, you are to take life for life, eye for eye, tooth for tooth, hand for hand, foot for foot, burn for burn, wound for wound, bruise for bruise' (Exod. 21:23-5).

Before condemning others, Christians should note that in the past thousand years, there have been more devastating wars among Christian states fighting each other than between Christian and Muslim states. And predominantly Christian states have killed more Jews and Muslims than predominantly Muslim states have killed Christians or Jews.[18]

Jesus treated the Hebrew Bible, our 'Old Testament', as his authority (Matt. 5:17-20). But he interpreted the Law according to the Prophets, especially Isaiah, whom he quoted at the start of his ministry (Luke 4). Jesus' devotion to peacemaking was inspired by Isaiah's vision for peace. Jesus knew by heart, 'how beautiful on the mountains are the feet of those who bring good news, who proclaim peace' (Is. 52:7). He knew a bringer of good news 'will not shout or cry out, or raise his voice in the streets - a bruised reed he will not break and a smouldering wick he will not quench' (Is. 42:2). The prayer for his people: 'no longer will violence be heard in your land, nor ruin or destruction within your borders' (Is. 60:18).

John the Baptist introduced Jesus at the beginning of his ministry as 'the Lamb of God who takes away the sin of the world' (John 1:29). We know the word 'Lamb' is not meant to be taken literally. Jesus was a 'man' not a 'Lamb'. However, the word 'Lamb' is used to describe the kind of 'man' he was. He was a 'Lamb' of a 'man' - pure and peaceable - not a duplicitous and dangerous wolf in sheep's clothing.

Jesus, the 'Lamb of God', sought to develop communities, of what he called 'flocks of sheep' at the grassroots (John 10:11-16). 'Sheep' was a seemingly innocuous but essentially counter-cultural term that Jesus used to describe people who lived with 'wolves' - those who preyed on other people - but who refused to become wolves themselves - even if it meant that the wolves might rip the flock to pieces because of their refusal to join the pack - and prey on others. 'I want you to live your lives as sheep, even in the midst of wolves.' said Jesus. 'Be shrewd. But always be harmless' (Matt. 10:16). 'Always treat other people as you would like them to treat you,' he said (Matt. 7:12). 'Even do good to those who do evil to you. Love those who hate you and bless those who curse you' (Matt. 5:44). 'Don't ever be afraid', he said to his flocks, 'of those who can kill the body, but can't kill your soul'. (Matt. 10:28)

Jesus argued for a different approach to that taken in the Mosaic law that legitimated retaliation. "You have heard that it was said, 'Eye for eye, and tooth for tooth.' But I tell you, Do not resist (or retaliate against) an evil person. If someone strikes you on the right cheek, turn to him the other also" (Matt. 5:38-9). Jesus told his disciples, 'you should always be ready to die - but never to kill - for your faith' (Matt. 16:24). So, under his guidance, the Jesus movement became a Jewish peace movement.[19]

For three centuries, Christianity was a completely pacifist movement. The Apostles taught Christians the pacifist principle: 'Love does no harm to its neighbour' (Rom. 13:10). Paul said too:

> Bless those who persecute you; bless and do not curse. Do not repay anyone evil for evil. Be careful to do what is right in the eyes of everybody. If it is possible, as far as it depends on you, live at peace with everyone. Do not take revenge. On the contrary: 'If your enem(ies) are hungry, feed

(them); if (they) are thirsty, give (them)
something to drink . . .' Do not be overcome
by evil, but overcome evil with good
(Rom. 12:14-21).

When Christianity became the official religion of the
Roman empire, Ambrose and Augustine developed a set of
criteria to call those in power – who make war – to be
accountable to the principles of justice. They argued that
in order for a war to be conducted according to the
principles of justice it would need to meet eight specific
conditions. One, it would need to be motivated by a 'just'
cause – and the only cause considered to be 'just' was to
stop the killing of large numbers of people. Two, it would
need to be administered by a 'just' authority – duly
constituted authorities had to proceed carefully according
to due process before taking action. Three, it would always
need to be a last resort – after all means of negotiation,
mediation, arbitration and non-violent sanctions had
been exhausted. Four, it would need to be for a 'just'
purpose – to secure the welfare, safety and security of all
parties in the dispute, including the enemy. Five, it would
need to be a reasonable risk – not a futile gesture, but a
realistic venture, with a reasonable hope of success. Six, it
would need to be cost-effective – the outcomes of victory
would outweigh the human costs of battle. Seven, that any
government intending to go to war should announce their
intentions – articulating the conditions that would need
to be met to avert it – in order to avoid going to war if at
all possible. Eight, that, if the war were to go ahead, not

only the ends, but also the means would need to be 'just' – non-combatants must be protected; once combatants surrender, they too must be protected from slaughter; and all prisoners must be protected from torture.

According to these criteria, our current wars are not 'just wars'. As Christians committed to peace and justice, we should robustly oppose these hostilities and actively seek reconciliation with our enemies.

Christ says that only committed 'peacemakers' have a legitimate claim to be called the 'children of God'.

8

Blessed are those who are persecuted
because of
righteousness

Blessed are those who are persecuted because of righteousness, for theirs is the kingdom of heaven.
(Matt. 5:10)

It is very important for us to be clear about what Jesus is not saying, before we consider what Jesus is saying. Jesus is not saying 'Blessed are those who are persecuted' as if there is some intrinsic merit in suffering persecution. Nowhere in the gospels does Jesus ever suggest that suffering – especially suffering persecution – is essentially meritorious or glorious at all. What Jesus does say is: 'Blessed are those who are persecuted because of righteousness' (Matt. 5:10). It is the willingness to suffer persecution 'because of righteousness' which is inherently worthwhile.

All through the gospels Jesus tells his disciples if they want to be righteous people in an unrighteous world, they will need to face the same inescapable certainty of systematic persecution as he did. Jesus says: 'I am the light of the world' (John 8:12) and 'You are the light of the world' as well (Matt. 5:14). Which, at first, seems wonderful; but, on second thoughts, is a role which has dreadful consequences. A light is not only a blaze, which attracts interest, but is also a radiance, which illuminates darkness. 'Everyone who does evil hates the light – because they do not want their evil deeds to be exposed' (John 3:20). People who 'do not want their evil deeds to be exposed' always do their best to crucify enlightened figures like Jesus and the good folk who seek to follow in their footsteps. So Jesus says to his disciples, 'If anyone would come after me, he must deny himself and take up his cross and follow me' (Matt. 16:24). He says

> Be warned. All people will hate you because of me . . . they will hand you over to the local councils and flog you in their synagogues. Brother will betray brother to death, and a father his child; children will rebel against their parents and have them put to death (Matt. 10:17–22).

We are not called to suffer, but to follow in the footsteps of Jesus. If suffering is necessary in order to do justice in the face of injustice, then so be it; the call to follow Jesus, in that case, is a call for us to suffer for righteousness in the same way as Jesus did. 'Christ suffered for you,' Peter wrote, 'leaving you an example that you might follow in his footsteps' (1 Pet. 2:21). The telling word in this sentence is the word Peter used in his letter for 'example'. It is *hupogrammos*, which indicates the perfect line of writing at the top of an exercise book, that anyone who wants to learn to write needs to learn to copy, as closely as they can. Thus, Peter is saying that when it comes down to it, we need to copy Christ as closely as we can - developing our capacity to suffer persecution for righteousness, like Christ.[20]

There are three things that we can achieve by our willingness to suffer persecution for righteousness: we can overcome evil; we can accomplish good; and we can witness powerfully to the way of Christ.

First, we can overcome evil. To be persecuted for righteousness is evil. When people do evil to us, the temptation is to return evil for evil. But that only serves to strengthen the stranglehold of evil in the world. So, we are explicitly instructed not to return evil for evil under any circumstances (Rom. 12:17). Instead of reacting to evil, we are expected to absorb evil, without reacting, and thus destroy its power. 'Do not resist evil. If someone strikes you on the right cheek, turn to him the other also' (Matt. 5:39).

As Gale Webbe says

> There are many ways to deal with evil. All of them are facets of the truth that the only ultimate way to conquer evil is to let it be smothered within a willing, living, human being. When it is absorbed there, like a spear into one's heart, it loses its power and goes no further. Those who 'turn the other cheek' when they are persecuted for righteousness, as Christ said, are blessed because

when they absorb the insult and the injury, 'like
a spear into one's heart,' the evil 'goes no further'.[21]

Second, we can accomplish good. In an evil world, we are only
ever free to do good, if we are prepared to suffer
persecution for righteousness. In our willingness to suffer
is our freedom to act. Jesus says, in a context where people
may kill you for doing the right thing, 'whoever wants to
save their life will lose it, but whoever loses their life for
me and for the gospel will save it' (Mark 8:35).

Viktor Frankl says what he observed as a Jewish psychiatrist
in a German concentration camp was, that if we compromise
our values in the hope of staying alive at any cost, we lose
our souls and become zombies; but if we have a steadfast
bottom line of righteousness we will not compromise – even
if it means being killed – we are blessed because we can be
true to ourselves and preserve our humanity.[22]

Third, we can witness powerfully to the way of Christ.
Someone dying for a cause doesn't make it right. But a
manifesto of love, written in blood, cannot be easily
dismissed. A movement which is worth dying for may lay
claim to be worth living for. Our suffering can reflect the
way of Christ that is the only beacon of hope for
compassion in the dark corners of our current pitiless
political economy.

Christ says that those of us who are 'persecuted because
of righteousness' are blessed, because, though we may not
be honoured for our quest for justice now, we will be
honoured in the world which is to come.

We can be
the change
we want to see

We can be the change we want to see in the world. But we can only do so by embodying the Be-Attitudes in the real world like Gladys Staines did.

How are we to go about doing this? Well, here are some suggestions.

First, find a version of the Be-Attitudes in a language that you can relate to. There are lots of different versions of the Bible these days. Look for a version which has the Be-Attitudes in words that speak to your heart. If you can't find one ready made, don't give up. Just do it yourself. Write your own version. Just make it true to the spirit of the scriptures. Then, when you've got your version of the Be-Attitudes, print out the text, and keep it somewhere where you can refer to it regularly.

Then select a Be-Attitude by asking yourself, 'Which Be-Attitude is relevant to my situation?'

After you have chosen a Be-Attitude that does this, meditate on what it says. 'What does this Be-Attitude tell me about the way I could relate to my situation?' Listen carefully to your heart for the answer to that question.

It may only take a few moments for you to get an answer to that question – but sometimes it may take you a few months. Don't give up. Hold the question in your heart and wait till your heart gives you an answer to your question. Then, once you have an idea of how to relate to your situation in a way that embodies the virtues in the Be-Attitudes, translate the Be-Attitude into action.

The Be-Attitudes confront us with truth straight from the heart of God. Nothing challenges our opinions and prejudices or calls us to a cause of pure compassion more than the Be-Attitudes.

To *quote* these Be-Attitudes is religious – but to *act* on them is revolutionary.

Whenever the Be-Attitudes are not translated into action they are reduced to meaningless clichés; a religious rhetoric about unrealized ideals that are worse than useless in a world which is sick and tired of a piety that refuses to roll its sleeves up and lend a hand to those in need.

But, whenever the Be-Attitudes are translated into action, the ideals become ideas that work; a divine agenda for radical – yet viable – personal growth and social change which enables us to work towards the realization of our dreams for a better world.

Each of us who feels inadequate needs to realize our capacity to act, and each of us who feels afraid needs to realize our courage to act. Each of us who feels impotent needs to recognize the potential of our actions, and each of us who feels insignificant needs to recognize the consequences of our actions.

Every act of truth is a victory over lies. Every act of love is a victory over hatred. Every act of justice is a victory over brutality. Every act of peace is a victory over bloodshed. And every risk a person takes to make a stand, no matter how small it may be, is a victory in the battle to build a better world.

So do the Be-Attitudes the best you can. Practise the love and justice which are the heart of the Be-Attitudes. Don't worry about making mistakes. Learn from your mistakes. Anything that's good enough to do is worth doing, even if we do it badly to begin with. But if we really want to do good, each time we do something, we should try to do it better. As they say: practice makes perfect!

Wecan.be

To enable us to help one another to 'be the revolution', we have set up a website.

The name of the website is www.wecan.be. The general aim of the website is to encourage one another to be the change we want to see in the world. The specific objective of the website is to encourage each other to adopt 'plan be' and practise the 'be-attitudes'. The explicit strategy is to use a web-based network to encourage one another to adopt Plan Be, practise the Be-Attitudes, and share our experiments in the change 'wecan.be'. We want to take as our texts the Be-Attitudes in Matthew 5 verses 1-12 (and Luke 6 verses 20-26) and as our mantra the quote from Mahatma Gandhi, 'We must be the change we want to see in the world.'

There are six ways we would like people to help one another through the website. We want people to

be inspired – through songs, images, quotes, etc.

be encouraged – through stories from round the world

be informed – through current news and views

be connected – through accompanying groups

be active – through practical campaigns

be reflective – through spirited meditations

So, people will need to send us quotes, songs, and images to 'be inspired'; stories, including your own, to 'be encouraged'; news, views, articles, and editorials to 'be informed'; names of groups of potential partners to 'be connected'; details of campaigns for peace, love, justice and sustainability to 'be active'; and lots of meditations to help us to 'be reflective' a bit more.

Our prayer is we can be the 'people-that-be' against the 'powers-that-be'.

Yet when I emailed my *Catholic Worker* friend, Jim Dowling, about the idea of the website, he replied

> Dave, I very much like the idea of getting Christians to recognize the importance of the beatitudes as guidelines on how to 'be'. But I really can't endorse the idea of something whose main demand is for people to sign a statement on the net. I may be wrong (always a first time), but I think it may be

> counter-productive, as it encourages people to believe they are actually doing something (when they are not). Once people could think they were resisting (the war) just by going to meetings. Now they can resist by going to meetings and being on the Internet. As much as I have started using this crazy machine I still claim the right to be cynical about it! Anyhow I hope it goes well, and one day I may be proven wrong. Jim.

I think that Jim makes a very valid point. Unless our *wecan.be* website actually encourages people to actively engage poverty and violence in the real world it will be worse than useless - it will be counter-productive.

We can only prove Jim wrong if we use the website as a creative resource for our do-it-yourself personal-political -spiritual revolution, not a substitute for it.

Some suggestions

Publicize the Be-Attitudes

In an article called 'Cold Turkey', Kurt Vonnegut, the famous satirical American author, wrote

> For some reason, the most vocal Christians among us never mention the beatitudes. But - often with tears in their eyes - they demand that the Ten Commandments be posted in public buildings and of course that's Moses, not Jesus. I haven't heard one of them demand that the Sermon on the Mount, the beatitudes, be posted anywhere.

I think it's time we took up Kurt's challenge, and posted the Be-Attitudes up everywhere we can.

I am mindful of how Luther's nailing of his Ninety-Five Theses for reform to the door of his church led to the reformation of his times; and I am of the mind that by posting a copy of the Be-Attitudes, not only in private spaces - like on the back of our bedroom door - but also in public spaces - like on the front of the door to our church, might lead to a new, and more radical, reformation - which not only preaches grace as a precept but also practises it as a process.

Some practical steps:

Discovering and/or creating as many different beautiful versions of the Be-Attitudes as we can

Posting your favourite version of the Be-Attitudes in a private space where you can see it - like on the back of your bedroom door

Posting your favourite version of the Be-Attitudes in a public space where others can see it - like on the front door of your church

Posting your favourite version of the Be-Attitudes on the *wecan.be* website

Develop Be-Attitudes support groups

Imagine what could happen if, instead of merely reciting our creeds, which (by and large) have little ethical content, we began every week by reciting - and reflecting on – the Be-Attitudes, with a focus on Christ-like ethical responses.

Imagine what could happen if our churches were transformed into spirited support groups that were committed to helping people live out the Be-Attitudes as an integrated step programme.

What AA groups have done for our addiction to alcohol, Be-Attitude groups could do for our addiction to status and violence. They could set us free to be fully human, fully alive, and fully active in loving our neighbours as ourselves!

We need to help one another to be the people we can be by:

Signing the pledge to practise the Be-Attitudes on the *wecan.be* website

Meditating on, acting, reflecting on and practising the Be-Attitudes yourself

Sharing your own experiences through the *wecan.be* website

Sending in quotes, songs, and images that inspired you to the *wecan.be* website so that others can be 'be inspired'

Sending in stories, including your own, so others can 'be encouraged'

Sending in news, views, articles, editorials, so others can 'be informed'

Sending in the names of groups of potential partners to 'be connected'

Sending in the details of campaigns for peace and justice to 'be active'

Sending in lots of meditations to help us to 'be reflective' a bit more

Using the *wecan.be* buttons, postcards and T-shirts to engage others

Wear the Be-Attitudes!

Kristin Jack writes about his experience of wearing a *wecan.be* T-shirt.

> When I first saw the T-shirts Craig had designed for Dave's 'plan be' campaign, I was impressed. This image of Jesus with fire in his eyes was so unlike that pasty Jesus (meek and mild) that adorns much religious art and when combined with the 'Be the revolution' slogan and the blood red background – *very powerful* I thought. I was excited, because it echoed the image of Jesus I first thrilled to when I was converted (all those years ago!) – but never could seem to find in any church.

> Well, two weeks ago I went off to the Micah network consultation in Thailand (Chang Mai), and decided to take eight shirts with me (hey, I was travelling light and living simply!). By day three I got around to wearing my one – and was immediately inundated with requests for them. They were especially popular with folk from South and Central America!! The parallels and contrasts with that other revolutionary (Ché I

Churches Advertising Network (contact The Revd Dr Tom Ambrose, The Vicarage, Trumpington, Cambridge CB2 2LH 01223 841262 / 07711263083.)

think his name was) creates a space for confrontation and then reflection. I love the contrasts: the revolution of violence vs the revolution of peace; revolution from the barrel of the gun vs the revolution from the heart of love and acts of service; the blood red colour that echoes the communist flag vs the blood sacrifice of Christ; and the wonderful catch cry: 'Be the revolution' vs 'make' or 'do' the revolution (i.e. we have to change first rather than enforce change on others) – wonderful echoes of the beatitudes in that. On the last day I had a brother from Chile begging me for my last shirt 'for Chile . . . for Chile . . . you have to'. So I took it off and gave it to him, with the warning to wash it immediately, as I had been wearing it two straight days!

Of course, the Jesus image is so striking it does have the power to polarize too. One guy walked past me (an older, white English male . . . coincidentally) and snarled 'I hate that T-shirt'. I stopped and asked why. 'Because Ché Guevara has nothing to do with Jesus.' So I pulled my shirt taut and pointed out that it was meant to be Jesus (crown of thorns and all). The guy wandered off muttering under his breath, clearly unhappy. But about half an hour later I passed him sitting at a table: he looked up, beamed and said, 'I love that T-shirt – where can I get one?' I guess the full contrasts and parallels of the images and message had begun to sink in, and caused him to examine his own gut reaction.

One person there who took a shirt (and then wore it continuously!) was a young woman who helped lead the worship for the conference (Australia's songwriter of the year 2001/2 (ballad and sacred song sections!) according to her album cover). On the last morning she called me over to thank me for the shirt. She then proceeded to say that if coming to the conference had been worth it for nothing else, it was worth it to get the shirt – which I thought was a bit over the top, but she unpacked what she meant by that for me: she and her mate had been wearing them up the street (the famous Chang Mai night market) and had had four serious and significant conversations with locals who had stopped them, asking her, 'That's Jesus isn't it?' One of them was a Burmese refugee, who they were able to link up with some Burmese delegates at the conference. This talented musician then asked me if it was OK for her to go back and write a song based on the 'be the revolution' slogan (for sure, I replied). Anyway, what I learnt from this was that the shirt makes an impact on a number of levels – the call to social justice and the call to evangelism levels for a start.

You may be wondering why I'm making such a big fuss about a T-shirt. I'll tell you why. I think that we have stumbled onto something disproportionately big here – something iconic and emblematic, a simple visual piece that has the power to arouse strong emotions and freight large amounts of meaning with just a few words and images, and every movement needs tools like this (songs, pictures, art, stories, etc.) if it hopes to have an impact beyond its immediate size (that is, to be prophetic and 'speak truth to power').

This is a powerful T-shirt. Let's put some serious prayer and thought into how we can use it most effectively and strategically and let's be the revolution!

Live the Be-Attitudes

Kristin Jack writes about what this means in his life:

> I work for Servants to Asia's Urban Poor, an evangelical mission. As evangelical Christians we are (or should be!) completely committed to the path of Jesus. Jesus is our Lord and absolute Master. His life of love is a template for how we should live. His words are the very Words of Life for us. Our theology is forged out of seeking to understand and obey all that Jesus has taught and asked of us.

> Jesus tells us that *if we obey* his teachings we *are* his disciples, and by so doing will find the truth – the truth about God, about ourselves, and about the world we live in (John 7:16-17 and 8:31-2). This truth will make us free. If we are truly following Jesus, we will be ignited by life's awe and mystery, enlarged by the giving and receiving of love and beauty, and empowered by the Spirit of God who animates and sustains the whole Universe (Heb. 1:1-4; Col. 2:2-3,9-10). We will learn to live with integrity and wholeness. As we follow Jesus we will change – and our world will be changed.

> As an evangelical mission, committed to bringing God's good news to the poor (Luke 4:17-21) and committed to being and making disciples wherever we go (Matt. 28:18-20), how do we in Servants try to show fidelity to the Sermon on the Mount and its beatitudes?

We set out to be a people who come close to and identify with the world's marginalized – the poor and poor in spirit, those who mourn and go hungry – and so we physically relocate to be with them. We are an incarnational mission, and so we are deliberately 'downwardly mobile'. Many of us have left affluent western lifestyles behind in order to live with the poor in the slums and ghettoes of Asia's cities.

We set out to be a people who hunger and thirst for justice and so we find ourselves working in places of darkness and oppression where the rich and powerful exploit the weak. We want to be those people of gentle strength (the meek) who get angry and fight to change these corrupt and evil systems, but without ever stooping to the use of violence (we can only overcome evil with good; we cannot overcome evil by mirroring it: Matt. 5:39/Rom. 12:21).

We set out to be a people of determined compassion, who offer hope in the midst of despair, peace-making in the midst of anguish, and courage in the midst of conflict. Simply, we want to be followers of Jesus.

This has led to a multitude of creative expressions: income generation, health projects, work with street kids and orphans, drug rehabilitation, community nutrition, therapeutic communities, local organizations, discipleship groups, urban poor churches, informal adult education, sanitation and recycling projects,

urban gardens, advocacy for land rights . . . but
more than anything else, it has led to getting
alongside people as friends and equals, as
colleagues and co-workers, in and for the
kingdom of God (Col. 4:11).

In Servants, we summarize this call to live out the
Sermon on the Mount with five key words that we
seek to practise:

1. *Incarnation* (living with the poor).
2. *Simplicity* (setting aside affluence and comfort).
3. *Community* (working with people and not just
   for them).
4. *Servanthood* (empowering not overpowering).
5. *Wholism* (proclaiming grace and promoting
   justice).

To be evangelical is to follow Jesus, nothing more
and nothing less. It is to join him in his revolution
of love and justice, compassion and peace, by
abandoning our own pursuit of wealth, status,
power or fame. It is to be more concerned about
lifting others up than perusing our own social or
material advancement. To be evangelical is to take
up Jesus' commission to go out into all the world,
to the poor, the lost and the hungry, and to invite
them also to be a part of this grace-full revolution.

This is what it means

Don't palm me off with civil religion
and your politely murmured prayers,
don't hand me your filthy mammon
or your barns of laundered cash.
Don't flatter me with pious words
catechisms so crisp and clean,
for I hate your victory chants
in praise of what I'm not:
your oh so personal idol,
middle class and mute.

But I am *not* silent
to those with ears to hear:
I weep, I groan, I scream,
and I am *so* weary
of your all too clever words
your rituals and your rhymes;
meaningless slick tokens
of power-point and song.

So once more I'm going to tell you
if you really want to hear,
for ***this*** is what it means
for ***this*** is what it means
to know me:

go love the Hungry One
with whom you must share your bread,
go welcome in The Stranger
who soils your silken bed,
go sit still beside the Tortured One

and hear his anguished cries,
go bathe the disfigured, Wretched One
caress His weeping skin,
bear up the abused, Abandoned One
bent beneath Her grief,
raise up the Fatherless One
eating scraps from off your street,

for **this** is what it means
for **this** is what it means
to know me.

(Inspired by Jer. 22:13–17 and Matt. 25:31–46)

Are you ready to live the Be-Attitudes?

You may not be called to live the beatitudes in the same way that Kristin is. But if you follow Christ, you are called to follow them in your circumstances. So let's commit ourselves to embodying the Be-Attitudes the best we can in our ordinary everyday lives and 'be the change we want to see' in the world. You might even want to sign:

The Be-Attitudes Pledge

I want to be the change I want to see . . .

1. I will identify with the poor 'in spirit'.

2. I will grieve over injustice in the world.

3. I will get angry, but never get aggressive.

4. I will seek to do justice, even to my enemies.

5. I will extend compassion to all those in need.

6. I will act with integrity, not for the publicity.

7. I will work for peace in the midst of violence.

8. I will suffer myself, rather than inflict suffering.

Signed . . . .   Date . . . .

Warning – We need to take the Be-Attitudes seriously; but we shouldn't take ourselves too seriously.

'Be purple!'
and other unhelpful commands

a reflection by Jarrod McKenna

*Be perfect, therefore, as your
heavenly Father is perfect.*
(Matt. 5:48)

Sitting with this text, what questions arise for you? Here are some that I have heard after teaching and workshopping it with many people:

- When Jesus tells us to 'be perfect' are we commanded to be something we can't?

- Is this some cruel trick from a mean god that sets us up to fail?

- Did Jesus have it all wrong about the God he called Abba and in fact when we ask for bread God does give us a stone?

- Is this just a punitive god having a laugh at the fact we are not created to be perfect yet we are commanded be so?

- Does this god just have dependency issues and this is his way of keeping himself in the picture by making us feel guilty that we weren't created angels so we turn to him?

- Are we told to be perfect just to drive home the fact that we suck but God has 'magic grace salve' that can make us feel better about being created to suck?

- Would it have been just as useful if we were commanded 'Be purple as your heavenly Father is purple', because both are impossible?

The logs in our eyes: the Impractical Paradigms

This kind of reading of Christ's teachings, although exaggerated here, is more common in our churches than we might think. 'The Impractical Paradigm' I see falling into two camps. Both treat Jesus' commands as 'ideals'. I find it interesting reflecting on my journey and the different churches I've been a part of and which camp they are flavoured with:

1. The 'must do' camp

The 'must do' camp read Christ's teachings as a legalistic must do to earn God's love and show we are 'real Christians'. This group is not restricted to quietist sects but can also be found in 'social-justice-Christian' types.

2. The 'can't do' camp

The 'can't do' camp reads Christ's teachings as insufferable ideals that make us realize we need grace because there is no way we can do what God asks. This group is not restricted to evangelicals but includes liberals as well (who sometimes think Jesus mistakenly thought it was the end of the world, and that's why he said to live such unrealistic things that we can now disregard).

Both of these readings produce fruit that is out of keeping with the good news of the reign of God:

- Both these readings can lead to joyless, death-dealing burdens that make discipleship oppressive or irrelevant and both are impotent.

- They lead to a distorted punitive image of God that looks nothing like our Lord Jesus.

- They also can lead to self-focused Christians. The focus on both these readings is either *my perfection* or *my depravity*. It's no wonder our churches are struggling with rampant consumerism. We've had Jesus sold to us as a product for, what Dallas Willard would call, 'sin management'. We've been told the gospel is all about me (!) instead of the gospel being about God's gracious deliverance in Christ by the in-breaking of the Kingdom.

- Both readings are individual and not communal in focus. Both often see salvation as something separate from a people and don't read the Sermon on the Mount primarily as the practices of a people supporting one another in the alternative to their former cycles and patterns of the world.

An alternative reading:
The Grace Participation Paradigm

One of the first empowering things we can do is ask about the context of the passage: what is the agenda of the writer of the gospel (because it's often not the agenda of the preacher). The context in that part of Matthew 5 is Jesus' teaching on enemy-love. Jesus is inviting us to proactively participate in God's transformational love.

Jesus is saying God's love is all-inclusive, not like the love of those who only love their friends or family. Jesus is saying God's love is unfailing in its action upon all our lives regardless of who we are or what we've done. Just as the sun is unfailing and indiscriminate in its rising on the evil and the good or the rain unfailing and indiscriminate in its falling on the just and unjust. So too God's gracious love acts upon us all. God's love is so radically and actively inclusive and all-embracing that even while we were enemies of God, God has taken the gracious action of sending his Son so that we can be reconciled. And we are empowered by the Spirit to participate in God's 'enemy-love' and therefore participate in the 'kingdom' – that is God's revolution, which is non-violently transforming not just us personally, but all of creation.

In relating to our enemies in the way God has related to us, we faithfully witness to God's chosen One and chosen Way, Jesus the non-violent Messiah. If taken seriously this will mean not trusting in our enemy's goodness but in the power of resurrection and God's love that conquers all. As Lee Camp would say this is not some naïve utopian dream that if we be nice to them they'll be nice to us. That might work in Barney's World [the purple dinosaur known for hugging kids and singing songs], but if we love with the very costly love seen in Christ we can expect to be treated by what has yet to be redeemed like he was (Lee Camp, from a lecture on the Sermon on the Mount given in the University Bible Class at Lipscomb University, 2001).

Not only has Jesus saved us from the vicious cycles of what has not been transformed, this grace empowers us to take part in God's revolution 'on earth as in heaven' which has broken into history in the person of Jesus. The black Baptist minister and civil rights hero Martin Luther King Jr. gave his life witnessing to the non-violence of Christ, in striving for an end to the unjust war he was living through, an end to poverty in the slums of America and around the world and an end to the treatment of black people as second-class citizens. He used to say repeatedly, 'No one is free if they fear death.' This is the irony of losing our lives in the gospel. Now that we've faced our fate as people of God's love in a world of violence, our lives are now free to be parables of God's love. Particularly by the way we relate to those we might otherwise exclude.

Then we get to verse 48 in chapter 5 of Matthew's Gospel. 'Be perfect . . . as your heavenly Father is perfect.' For a Jewish audience it's clearly a reference to Leviticus 19:2, 'Be holy because I, the LORD your God, am holy.' It is clearly a call to *imitatio Dei* (imitation of God) but what is this God like that we are to imitate?

Many theologians have moved from reading Plato and Aristotle and have returned to verse 48 and have read into the word 'perfect' the Greek idealism of the philosophers. Many liberal scholars today want to pass Jesus off as a wisdom teacher like the Cynics and say he's teaching us to have the moral perfectionism of this stagnant Greek deity that functions as an ideal somewhere off in the distance. This however is a completely foreign way of thinking about God for Jesus if we are going to take his context (remember 'a text without a context is a sign your being conned') and therefore his Jewishness seriously.

It would hardly make sense for Jesus in verse 47 to be criticizing the way pagans (non-Jews) include only people like themselves among those they love, and then in verse 48 to extol pagan ways of thinking! The word translated perfect in Matthew 5:48 is *teleios* meaning 'having reached its end' or 'complete'. This is why biblical scholars like Glen Stassen are suggesting Matthew 5:48 can more helpfully be translated, 'Be complete [in love] as your heavenly Father is complete [in love].' Not only is it practical, it fits the context of the passage with much more integrity than any weird command to be something we can't (like be purple!!). It also fits with Luke's teaching on loving our enemies, where the crescendo is 'be merciful as your Father is merciful' or 'be compassionate as your Father is compassionate'.

The Grace Participation Paradigm: a practical holiness

For the Pharisees, holiness was a matter of excluding. Excluding the prostitute, excluding the leper, excluding the tax collector, excluding the demon-possessed and the unclean. Many of us have seen churches today where people who are pushed to the margins of society are also kept at the margins of faith communities. Yet in Jesus we see a God who includes zealot and tax collector, Greek and Jew, slave and free, female and male. While others exclude in the interest of 'holiness', Matthew and Luke both suggest that holiness is transfigured in Jesus. The practice of enemy-love is the practice of the holiness of God's revolution or 'kingdom', where outsiders are not shunned but welcomed, held and healed in transforming ways. Jesus provides for us a *grace participation paradigm*, where though we are sinners, God's unfailing love shines and rains on us and we are invited to live God's grace in the way we relate to all others, to be complete and all-inclusive in transformational love just as our God is. Instead of killing, hiding or suffocating what is impure, weak or dreaded by us in ourselves, in our churches, in our communities and in our world, God holds all of it to be transformed. Even us. And we are not just saved from our old ways: we're saved into a people who by God's grace are invited into the dynamic deliverance that participation in God's gracious reign, or kingdom.

The good news of Jesus is that new life is found not in 'must do' or 'can't do' but in the reality that 'God does' through us what we were created for by God's grace! Our world, living through an unjust war and the destruction of God's good earth at a rate never before seen in history, desperately needs people who embody such a fearless, redemptive, 'perfect' love.

Jarrod McKenna is the co-ordinator of EPYC – Empowering Peacemakers in Your Community. Jarrod says, 'The above are some frameworks EPYC has developed for Christians to unpack how they have experienced Christ's teachings being taught. EPYC's interactive workshops and retreats draw heavily on the biblical scholarship of a number of people, including Lee Camp, Walter Wink and Glen Stassen, all of which I recommend to anyone wanting to explore this deeper. Here end the ads.'

Notes

1 Bruce Lincoln, *Holy Terrors* (Chicago: University of Chicago Press, 2002).

2 Greg Austin, Todd Kranock and Thom Oommen, *God and War* (Bradford: Department of Peace Studies, 2003).

3 In 1993, the Parliament of the World's Religions was convened in Chicago, with 8,000 people from all over the world coming together to see if they could find a common ethic in their religious traditions that they could use to address the issue of violence, and they came up with the Golden Rule.

4 Peter Singer, *One World* (Melbourne: Text Publishing, 2002).

5 Dorothee Soelle, *Suffering* (Philadelphia: Fortress Press, 1975), p. 73.

6 William Barclay, *The Gospel of Matthew*, vol. 1, The Daily Study Bible (Edinburgh: Saint Andrew Press, 1956), pp. 91-2.

7 Glen Stassen and David Gushee, *Kingdom Ethics* (Downers Grove: InterVarsity Press, 2003), p. 134.

8 Os Guinness, *The Dust of Death* (Downers Grove: InterVarsity Press, 1973), p. 384.

9 Swami Agnivesh, 'Healing the Spirit of Gladys Staines', www.swamiagnivesh.com

10 'Forgiveness Brings Healing', www.lifepositive.com

11 'I Am Overwhelmed: Gladys Staines', *The Hindu*, New Delhi, 28 March 2006, www.hinduonthenet.com

12 Swami Agnivesh, 'Healing the Spirit of Gladys Staines', www.swamiagnivesh.com

13 Glen Stassen and David Gushee, *Kingdom Ethics* (Downers Grove: InterVarsity Press, 2003), pp. 355ff.

14 For more on what this means, see the article '"Be Purple" and Other Unhelpful Commands' in the Appendix.

15 Dallas Willard, *The Divine Conspiracy* (San Francisco: Harper, 1998), pp. 146ff.

16 Glen Stassen and David Gushee, *Kingdom Ethics* (Downers Grove: InterVarsity Press, 2003), pp. 135ff.

17 Glen Stassen and David Gushee, *Kingdom Ethics* (Downers Grove: InterVarsity Press, 2003), p. 142.

18 'Alive and Kicking', *New Internationalist*, August 2004.

19 Glen Stassen and David Gushee, *Kingdom Ethics* (Downers Grove: InterVarsity Press, 2003), p. 152.

20 William Barclay, *The Letters of Peter*, The Daily Study Bible (Edinburgh: Saint Andrew Press, 1959), p. 95.

21 G. Webbe, *The Night and Nothing* (New York: Seabury Press, 1964), p. 109.

22 Viktor Frankl, *Man's Search for Meaning* (New York: Simon & Schuster, 1963).

Battles Christians Face
Vaughan Roberts

'The Christian life is victorious, full of joy and triumph.'

Well, usually.

Sometimes.

Ever?

The Bible is clear that the Christian's hope and faith are forged in the fiery battles of life. Suffering and temptation shape and strengthen us. But in the twenty-first century many of the crucial difficulties that Christians have always struggled with are lightly treated by some . . .

How can I approach feelings of lust in a godly way when 'lust' is now an alluring name for perfume or chocolate?

How can I battle guilt with integrity when friends encourage me to believe that sin doesn't really exist?

Why do I feel so depressed when the impression is often given that Christians should always have a smile on their face and in their heart?

In *Battles Christians Face* bestselling author **Vaughan Roberts** equips us with practical weapons to face our daily battles with confidence – including those above, and others. The teaching of this book restores our hope of living godly lives here and now – lives that honour and bear witness to Jesus Christ.

ISBN: 978-185078-728-0

*Available on **www.authenticmedia.co.uk** or from your local Christian bookshop*

Stories from China: Fried Rice for the Soul
Luke Wesley

'I hope that everyone who desires to help the Chinese Church, whether living overseas or serving in China, might have a chance to read this book.' Brother Yun

Stories from China is a collection of 52 inspirational stories that seek to illustrate the strength of the Chinese Church and convey the significant insights it offers to Christians in the West. A brief, introductory chapter gives a general overview of the Church in China and provides important context for the stories that follow. Each story is prefaced with a Scripture reading and concludes with a prayer. The book offers perspective on Chinese culture and Christianity, as well as devotional insights. *Stories from China* is written for the general reader and will be meaningful to people from a wide range of denominational backgrounds.

Luke Wesley has lived and served in China for the past ten years. He is fluent in Mandarin Chinese and has ministered extensively in house church and TSPM church settings. He has helped establish a small network of house churches and currently serves as the director of an underground, residential Bible school in China that he founded.

ISBN: 978-185078-638-2

*Available on **www.authenticmedia.co.uk** or from your local Christian bookshop*

Learning at the Crossroads
Neil Hood

'Balanced, practical and inspiring. Full of spiritual common sense.'
Adrian Plass

Have you ever stood at crossroads and wondered which way to turn? Knowing that choosing one particular path in these areas will change you and the pattern of your life?

Sometimes we're too impulsive in making our choices. Most of us fumble through life's decisions without ever thinking of asking God what his route for our life is. Taking the Bible's wise advice, the experiences of biblical characters, contemporary stories and a wealth of personal experience, Neil Hood guides us back to God.

Written in a clear, accessible style, *Learning at the Crossroads* has practical questions in each section to help you apply these truths to your own situation.

Stop. Look. Listen. Read.

'Looking for an MOT test for your life? Neil Hood provides us all with incisive, vital questions. And he writes from the crossroads himself. Tender, authentic, and laced with grace.' Jeff Lucas, author, speaker, broadcaster

'I predict this book will be the spiritual manual for Christians in the 21st century as we endeavour to live out our faith in the complexities of so called post-modernity where all is flux and nothing is certain.' Tony Sargent, International Christian College

'Full of spiritual wisdom, Neil's writing is marked by a rare honesty.' Derek Tidball, London School of Theology

ISBN: 978-85978-641-2

*Available on **www.authenticmedia.co.uk** or from your local Christian bookshop*

True Grit
Deborah Meroff

A wake-up call to crises facing women around the world, told through the exciting stories of nine courageous people and hard-hitting 'Vital Statistics' files.

This tells the inspiring true adventures of nine 'ordinary' women who are making a difference in such places as Tajikistan, India and Lebanon. We hear about Kathryn, a deaf American who built a ministry to the deaf in Israel; Pam, who lived and worked in war-racked Tajikstan, a country completely alien and unknown to Westerners; and Cindy who ended up returning as a missionary to Vietnam, a country from which she had had a dangerous escape as a teenager.

Fact files between stories highlight global female abuse, such as child brides, sex trafficking, girl soldiers and 'honour' killings. But the book does not stop there. *True Grit* goes on to point out simple ways for all of us to help turn the tide for women worldwide.

Deborah Meroff has travelled to over eighty countries in the last eighteen years in her role of journalist-at-large for the mission organisation, Operation Mobilisation. She has written several books, plus dozens of articles in several countries and is a columnist for *Woman Alive* magazine.

ISBN: 978-85078-575-0

*Available on **www.authenticmedia.co.uk** or from your local Christian bookshop*